LOLA
THE
LOGGERHEAD

TULSA

ISBN: 978-1-954095-34-2

Lola the Loggerhead

Yorkshire Publishing
1425 E 41st Pl
Tulsa, OK 74105
www.YorkshirePublishing.com
918.394.2665

Published in the USA

LOLA

THE

LOGGERHEAD

A Story About Loggerhead Sea Turtles

December 2021

Chandler,
Merry Christmas!
And don't forget
to Dream BIG!!
:)

Adrienne Palma

By

Adrienne Palma

To Michael, David, Chris, and Ann

Dream BIG

Foreword

A delightful story of the beautiful loggerhead sea turtles that return to the beaches of the Outer Banks each summer to lay their eggs...as well as a tribute to the Network for Endangered Sea Turtles (N.E.S.T.) that protects, promotes and saves many sea turtles each year.

Dr. Holly Robinson
Vice-President
N.E.S.T. Board

Hi, I'm Lola, a loggerhead sea turtle.
Come along as I tell you my story.

It was on the coast of North Carolina, in a place
known as the Outer Banks.

I was born on the shores of Nags Head,
a town along the Atlantic Ocean.

It was here that my mom laid her eggs thirty years ago.
A loggerhead sea turtle returns to the same general area
where she was hatched to lay her eggs. Isn't that amazing!!!

After we hatched, my siblings and I quickly headed for the water. Upon entering the water, we swam very fast! Some hatchlings are eaten by ghost crabs and birds as they emerge from the nests, so we moved swiftly. As hatchlings, loggerhead sea turtles are only the size of Oreo™ cookies with flippers! We are tiny, but very determined to get to the water! Unfortunately, many hatchlings are snatched up easily by big fish when they enter the ocean. These big fish are considered predators.

Once we were in the water, my sister, Lucy, and I swam together! We swam to the Gulf Stream where the water is really warm. The Gulf Stream is a fast moving ocean current that begins in the Gulf of Mexico and flows into the Atlantic Ocean. We hide in the sea weed to escape being eaten because hatchlings are food for predators in the ocean. Then we kept swimming until we reached an area in the Atlantic Ocean called the Sargasso Sea. Have you noticed the "heart" birthmark on my forehead? I cannot see it, but Lucy told me about it. Lucy says it makes her happy to see it everyday. Every loggerhead has something unique about them. I am glad mine is a beautiful heart. I am heart happy.

Loggerheads love the ocean, however, we have to be very careful of getting hit by boats, getting stuck with fish hooks, or getting entangled in fishing nets.

The ocean is a busy place!!! We just want to stay safe and swim! Hatchlings can swim up to one mile an hour for a short distance. As adults, we can swim up to 15 miles an hour, usually for catching food or escaping predators.

Lucy and I race each other to catch our food!!!

As a hatchling, I was an omnivore, which means I used to feed on plants and animals. Now that I am an adult, I am considered a carnivore. That means I eat animals. I have a huge head and super strong jaws so that I can eat lots of sea creatures. I like to eat crabs, horseshoe crabs, conchs, whelks, shrimp, fish, sea cucumbers, mussels and lots of other sea life. Crabs are my favorite! Lucy loves shrimp! There are lots of plastic bags and popped balloons in the water. I have to be very careful not to eat them.

I am now swimming back to Nags Head to lay my eggs.
It is after dark when I lumber my way
out of the water onto the sand.
I drag myself up the beach looking for a place to dig my nest.
With my back flippers, I hollow out a pit.
The hole must be deep enough for all of my eggs.

I laid 100 eggs!
After that, I use my back flippers again to cover the eggs.
Then I fling more sand around to erase any sign of the nest.

After covering up the hole, I make my way back to the water.
I am so tired.
It is still dark. I can see the moon
shining over the calm waters.
I am finally back in the water.
It is time to swim away from the shore,
leaving my eggs behind.

In the Outer Banks of North Carolina, there
is an organization called N.E.S.T.
that looks after loggerhead sea turtle nests.
N.E.S.T. stands for the Network for Endangered Sea Turtles.
I am really glad they do!
The N.E.S.T. volunteers keep a watch out for
new loggerhead sea turtle nests.
When they find a nest, they put tape
around the area to protect it.
They keep really good records of the nests that
are along the beaches of the Outer Banks!

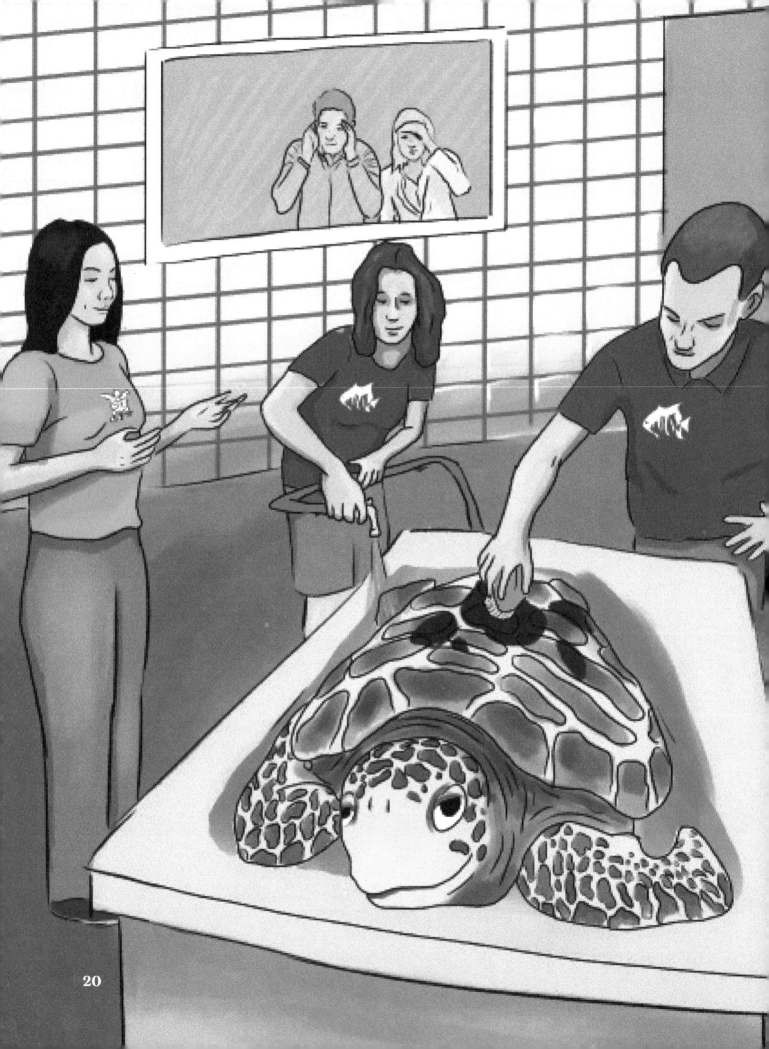

The N.E.S.T. volunteers also work closely with the staff at the Sea Turtle Assistance and Rehabilitation (STAR) Center at the NC Aquarium on Roanoke Island. The STAR Center cares for sick and injured sea turtles. The staff takes really good care of the sea turtles. Visitors can see these sea turtles through viewing windows. Many sea turtles are returned back to the ocean each year.

It will take about 60 days for the eggs to hatch.
The N.E.S.T. volunteers, JoAnn, Tony, and
Christine, keep a close watch on my nest.
They install fancy thermometers in the
nest to collect data about my eggs.
On their Smartphones, they can read graphs which give
lots of good data to how my eggs are developing. The
data is recorded in a log. These volunteers keep very
good notes about loggerhead nests. A big THANK YOU to
these volunteers for protecting us and keeping us safe!

The N.E.S.T. volunteers really enjoy talking with
children and adults who walk along the beach.
They love to share information about loggerhead sea turtles.
One day JoAnn and Christine were watching my
nest. Stella and her brother CJ walked by.
These N.E.S.T. volunteers told them all about me and my nest.
They had some posters and bookmarks
to share with the children too.
Stella and CJ live in Nags Head, not too far from the nest.
They come back every night to check on the nest!
They cannot wait to see the hatchlings!

Finally one night, after 60 days, it happens!
The N.E.S.T. volunteers, along with Stella and
CJ, see some movement in the sand!
It is called a "boil" when the sand begins to toss
around as the hatchlings work their way out!
The group watch in the dark as the
hatchlings crawl out of their eggs.

The hatchlings quickly climb out of the nest!
Stella and CJ gaze in wonder as these beautiful
creatures scamper to the water!
No flashlights are used. The hatchlings can
see the white of the waves and that is
the direction they head towards. And the smell
of the ocean and heading down hill usually
helps them too.
After all of the hatchlings were in the water,
everyone hugged each other and gave high 5's.
Stella said, "I hope they swim safely out to sea."
CJ replied, "Me too!"
JoAnn explained, "It will take them two
days to reach the Gulf Stream.
Predators in the ocean want to eat them. Unfortunately, only
one in one hundred loggerheads make it to the Gulf Stream.
But we know Mother Nature takes care of her babies."

As for me, I am now swimming along the
eastern coast with my sister Lucy again.
I am thirty years old and hope to live a long time.
Me and my happy heart. That is what life is all about!
The water is still warm and very calm.
Lucy and I are racing to see who can
catch some fish for dinner!

Fun Facts

a. The average lifespan for loggerheads is 47-67 years.

b. Loggerheads are named for their massive heads (which look like a big log!) and strong jaws. The average weight is 180-300 pounds.

c. Loggerheads nest several times in the season. Usually, there are 12-17 days between each nest. They average about 120 eggs per nest.

d. Leatherback turtles are bigger than loggerheads but have soft shells.

e. Loggerheads enjoy eating whelks and conch shells. Their strong teeth and powerful jaws crunch right through the shells!

f. The temperature of the developing eggs determines the gender of the loggerheads. This is known as temperature-dependent sex determination (TSD).

g. After the loggerheads hatch and make it to the water, they are completely adapted to life in the ocean. Only the females come ashore to dig their nests and deposit the eggs.

h. The Network for Endangered Sea Turtles (N.E.S.T.) is a non profit organization dedicated to the preservation and protection of the habitats and migration routes of Sea Turtle and other marine animals on the Outer Banks of North Carolina from the Virginia border to Nags Head.

i. The Sea Turtle Assistance and Rehabilitation (STAR) Center at the NC Aquarium on Roanoke Island cares for sick and injured sea turtles.

j. The Endangered Species Act of 1973 was enacted to protect endangered and threatened species and their habitats.

k. The Continental Shelf is the edge of a continent that lies under the ocean.

l. The Gulf Stream is a strong ocean current that brings warm water from the Gulf of Mexico into the Atlantic Ocean. It extends all the way up the eastern coast of the United States and Canada.

m. The Sargasso Sea is located in the middle of the North Atlantic Ocean and is completely surrounded by water on all sides. It is unique because it is defined only by ocean currents.

n. *Author's Note - Loggerhead sea turtles are solitary creatures. For the purpose of this story, liberties were taken to have Lola and Lucy stay together.*

References and Resources

1. Network for Endangered Sea Turtles
   http://www.nestonline.org/

2. North Carolina Aquarium on Roanoke Island
   http://www.ncaquariums.com/roanoke-island
   http://www.ncaquariums.com/roanoke-island-whats-new/category/star-center

3. Loggerhead Sea Turtles
   https://www.nationalgeographic.com/animals/reptiles/l/loggerhead-sea-turtle/#:~:tex-t=Loggerhead%20turtles%20are%20the%20most%20abundant%20of%20all,on%20the%20threatened%20species%20list%20since%201978.%20Habitat
   https://www.natgeokids.com/au/discover/animals/sea-life/loggerhead-turtle-facts/
   https://www.nationalgeographic.com/animals/reptiles/l/loggerhead-sea-turtle/
   www.fisheries.noaa.gov/species/loggerhead-turtle
   herpsofnc.org/loggerhead/
   www.natgeokids.com/au/discover/animals/sea-life/loggerhead-turtle-facts/seaturtle.org/

4. Continental Shelf
   https://www.nationalgeographic.org/encyclopedia/continental-shelf/

5. Gulf Stream
   https://scijinks.gov/gulf-stream/

6. Endangered Species Act of 1973
   https://www.fws.gov/international/laws-treaties-agreements/us-conservation-laws/en-dangered-species-act.html

7. Sargasso Sea
   https://oceanservice.noaa.gov/facts/sargassosea.html

Acknowledgements

Heartfelt thanks to the following people who were instrumental in making this book a reality. I am truly humbled by your support. It has been invaluable and is appreciated. Thank you for making this dream come true!

- Louise Vance, Holly Robinson, and the dedicated members of the Network for Endangered Sea Turtles. You are the unsung heroes! Louise, thank you for your quick replies to my countless emails!!! Holly, thank you for writing the Foreword!!!

- Larry Warner, Alexandra Jeddry, and the hardworking employees at the North Carolina Aquarium on Roanoke Island. The care given to the loggerhead sea turtles at the STAR Center is amazing!

- Barbara and John Sbunka for reading the story and offering great suggestions. The story is richer because of your input!

- Christian Legner for the resources and great input.

- Stella and CJ Price, I am SO glad you are a part of this book. The illustrations capture your spirit and amazing personalities!

- The team at Yorkshire Publishing. You have been the BEST to work with again! May each book in the *Under the Sea* series be as exciting and fun to bring to life as *Lola*!!!

To you readers, thank you for selecting this book. May learning about loggerhead sea turtles bring an awareness in keeping these beautiful creatures safe for many years to come. The writing of this book and the upcoming books in the *Under the Sea series* let me live my dream everyday. Dream BIG...then make it happen.

Coming Soon ... the 2nd book in the *Under the Sea* series:

Shalim the Shark
A Story about Sand Tiger Sharks
by Adrienne Palma